GIVING ALMS, NO CHARITY

DANIEL DEFOE

RE-ISSUED IN A SERIES OF REPRINTS OF
CLASSIC ENGLISH WORKS ON
THE HISTORY AND DEVELOPMENT OF
ECONOMIC THOUGHT,
UNDER THE EDITORIAL DIRECTION OF
PROFESSOR W. E. MINCHINTON
UNIVERSITY OF EXETER

S. R. PUBLISHERS LIMITED
JOHNSON REPRINT CORPORATION

This reproduction has been made with the kind permission of the Goldsmiths' Librarian, University of London, from the copy held in the Goldsmiths' Library, Senate House, London, W.C. 1.

Mar., 1971

The publishers would like to acknowledge the assistance of Dr. J. H. P. Pafford, M.A., F.S.A., F.L.A., the former Goldsmiths' Librarian, Miss M. B. C. Canney of the Goldsmiths' Library and Mr. F. J. Bosley, M.I.R.T., the chief photographer to the Goldsmiths' Library, without whose assistance this series of reprints could not have been successfully under taken.

Library of Congress Catalog Card Number: 75-114077

British Standard Book Number: 85409-248-X

S. R. Publishers Ltd.
East Ardsley, Wakefield
Yorkshire, England

Johnson Reprint Corporation
111 Fifth Avenue
New York, N.Y. 10003, U.S.A.

Printed in the U.S.A.

Giving Alms no Charity,

And Employing the

P O O R

A Grievance to the

N A T I O N,

Being an

E S S A Y

Upon this

𝕲𝖗𝖊𝖆𝖙 𝕼𝖚𝖊𝖘𝖙𝖎𝖔𝖓,

Whether Work-houfes, Corporations, and Houfes of
Correction for Employing the Poor, as now pra-
ctis'd in *England*; or Parifh-Stocks, as propos'd in
a late Pamphlet, Entituled, *A Bill for the better Relief, Imployment and Settlement of the Poor*, &c. Are
not mifchievous to the Nation, tending to the Deftruction of our Trade, and to Encreafe the Number and Mifery of the Poor.

Addreffed to the Parliament of England.

L O N D O N:

Printed, and Sold by the Bookfellers of *London* and *Weft-
minfter*. MDCCIV.

To the Knights, Citizens and Burgesses in Parliament Assembled.

Gentlemen,

HE that has Truth and Justice, and the Interest of *England* in his Design, can have nothing to fear from an *English* Parliament.

This makes the Author of these Sheets, however Despicable in himself, apply to this Honourable House, without any Apology for the Presumption.

Truth, *Gentlemen*, however meanly dress'd, and in whatsoever bad Company she happens to come, was always entertain'd at your Bar; and the Commons of *England* must cease to act like themselves, or which is worse, like their Ancestors, when they cease to entertain any Proposal, that offers it self at their Door, for the general Good and Advantage of the People they Represent

I willingly grant, That 'tis a Crime in good Manners to interrupt your more weighty Councils, and disturb your Debates; with empty nauseous Trifles in Value, or mistaken Schemes and whoever ventures to Address You, ought to be well assur'd he is in the right, and that the Matter suits the Intent of your meeting, *viz. To dispatch the weighty Affairs of the Kingdom.*

And as I have premis'd this, so I freely submit to any Censure this Honourable Assembly shall think I deserve, if I have broke in upon either of these Particulars.

I have but one Petition to make with respect to the Author, and that is, That no freedom of Expression, which the Arguments may oblige him to, may be construd as a want of Respect, and a breach of the due Deference every *English* Man owes to the representing Power of the Nation.

It would be hard, that while I am honestly offering to your Consideration something of Moment for the general Good, Prejudice

judice fhould lay Snares for the Author, and private Pique make him an Offender for a Word.

Without entring upon other Parts of my Chara&ter, 'tis enough to acquaint this Affembly, that I am an *Englifh* Freeholder, and have by that a Title to be concern'd in the good of that Community of which I am an unworthy Member.

This Honourable Houfe is the Reprefentative of all the Freeholders of *England*; you are Affembl'd for their Good, you ftudy their Intereft, you poffefs their Hearts, and you hold the Strings of the general Purfe.

To you they have Recourfe for the Redrefs of all their Wrongs, and if at any time one of their Body can offer to your Affiftance, any fair, legal, honeft and rational Propofal for the publick Benefit, it was never known that fuch a Man was either rejeéted or difcourag'd.

And on this Account I crave the Liberty to affure you, That the Author of this feeks no Reward; to him it fhall always be Reward enough to have been capable of ferving his native Country, and Honour enough to have offer'd fomething for the publick Good worthy of Confideration in your Honourable Affembly.

Pauper Vbique jacet, faid our famous Queen *Elizabeth*, when in her Progrefs thro' the Kingdom fhe faw the vaft Throngs of the Poor, flocking to fee and blefs her; and the Thought put her Majefty upon a continu'd ftudy how to recover her People from that Poverty, and make their Labour more profitable to themfelves in Particular, and the Nation in General.

This was eafie then to propofe, for that many ufeful Manufaétures were made in foreign Parts, which our People bought with *Englifh* Money, and Imported for their ufe.

The Queen, who knew the Wealth and vaft Numbers of People which the faid Manufaétures had brought to the neighbouring Countries then under the King of *Spain*, the *Dutch* being not yet Revolted, never left off endeavouring what fhe happily brought to pafs, *viz.* the tranfplanting into *England* thofe Springs of Riches and People.

She faw the *Flemings* prodigioufly Numerous, their Cities ftood thicker than her Peoples Villages in fome parts; all forts of ufeful Manufaétures were found in their Towns, and all their People were

were rich and busie, no Beggars, no Idlenefs, and confequently no want was to be feen among them.

She faw the Fountain of all this Wealth and Workmanfhip, I mean the Wool, was in her own Hands, and *Flanders* became the Seat of all thefe Manufactures, not becaufe it was naturally Richer and more Populous than other Countries, but becaufe it lay near *England*, and the Staple of the *Englifh* Wool which was the Foundation of all their Wealth, was at *Antwerp* in the Heart of that Country.

From hence, it may be faid of *Flanders*, it was not the Riches and the number of People brought the Manufactures into the *Low Countries*, but it was the Manufactures brought the People thither, and Multitudes of People make Trade, Trade makes Wealth, Wealth builds Cities, Cities Enrich the Land round them, Land Enrich'd rifes in Value, and the Value of Lands Enriches the Government.

Many Projects were fet on foot in *England* to Erect the Woollen Manufacturer here, and in fome Places it had found Encouragement, before the Days of this Queen, efpecially as to making of Cloath, but Stuffs, Bays, Says, Serges, and fuch like Wares were yet wholly the Work of the *Flemings*.

At laft an Opportunity offer'd perfectly unlook'd for, viz. The Perfecution of the Proteftants, and introducing the *Spanifh* Inquifition into *Flanders*, with the Tyranny of the Duke *D'Alva*.

It cannot be an ungrateful Obfervation, here to take notice how Tyranny and Perfecution, the one an Oppreffion of Property, the other of Confcience, always Ruine Trade, Impoverifh Nations, Depopulate Countries, Dethrone Princes, and Deftroy Peace.

When an *Englifh* Man reflects on it, he cannot without infinite Satisfaction look up to Heaven, and to this Honourable Houfe, *that* as the fpring, *this* as the Stream *from* and *by* which the Felicity of this Nation has obtain'd a Pitch of Glory, Superior to all the People in the World.

Your Councils efpecially, when bleft from Heaven, *as now we truft they are*, with Principles of Unanimity and Concord, can never fail to make Trade Flourifh, War Succefsful, Peace certain,

tain, Wealth flowing, Bleffings probable, the Queen Glorious, and the People Happy.

Our unhappy Neighbours of the *Low Countries* were the very Reverfe of what we *blefs our felves for in You.*

Their Kings were Tyrants, their Governours Perfecutors, their Armies Thieves and Blood-hounds.

Their People Divided, their Councils Confus'd, and their Miferies Innumerable.

D'Alva the *Spanifh* Governor, Befieg'd their Cities, Decimated the Inhabitants, Murther'd their Nobility, Profcrib'd their Princes and Executed 18000 Men by the Hand of the Hang-man.

Confcience was trampl'd under foot, Religion and Reformation hunted like a Hare upon the Mountains, the Inquifition threatned, and Foreign Armies introduc'd.

Property fell a Sacrifice to Abfolute Power, the Countrey was Ravag'd, the Towns Plunder'd, the Rich Confifcated, the Poor Starv'd, Trade Interrupted, and the 10*th.* Penny demanded.

The Confequence of this was, *as in all Tyrannies and Perfecutions it is,* the People fled and fcatter'd themfelves in their Neighbours Countries, Trade languifh'd, Manufactures went abroad, and never return'd, Confufion reign'd, and Poverty fucceeded.

The Multitude that remain'd, pufh'd to all Extremities, were forc'd to obey the Voice of Nature, and in their own juft Defence to take Arms againft their Governours.

Deftruction it felf has its ufes in the World, the Afhes of one City Rebuilds another, and God Almighty, who never acts in vain, brought the Wealth of *England,* and the Power of *Holland* into the World from the Ruine of the *Flemifh Liberty.*

The *Dutch* in defence of their Liberty revolted, renounc'd their Tyrant Prince, and profper'd by Heaven and the Affiftance of *England,* erected the greateft Common-wealth in the World.

Innumerable Obfervations would flow from this part of the prefent Subject, but Brevity is my ftudy, I am not teaching; for I know who I fpeak to, but relating and obferving the Connexion of Caufes, and the wonderous Births which *lay then* in the Womb of Providence, and are fince come to life.

Particularly how Heaven directed the Oppreffion and Tyranny of the Poor fhould be the Wheel to turn over the great Machine of Trade from *Flanders* into *England.*   And

And how the Perfecution and Cruelty of the *Spaniards* againft Religion fhould be directed by the fecret Over-ruling Hand, to be the Foundation of a People, and a Body that fhould in Ages then to come, be one of the chief Bulwarks of that very Liberty and Religion they fought to deftroy.

In this general Ruine of Trade and Liberty, *England* made a Gain of what fhe never yet loft, and of what fhe has fince encreas'd to an inconceivible Magnitude.

As *D'Alva* worried the poor *Flemings*, the Queen of *England* entertain'd them, cherifh'd them, invited them, encourag'd them. Thoufands of innocent People fled from all Parts from the Fury of this Mercilefs Man, and as *England* to her Honour has always been the Sanctuary of her diftrefs'd Neighbours, fo now fhe was fo to her fpecial and particular Profit.

TheQueen who faw the Opportunity put into her hands which fhe had fo long wifh'd for, not only receiv'd kindly the Exil'd *Flemings*, but invited over all that would come, promifing them all poffible Encouragement, Priviledges and Freedom of her Ports, and the like.

This brought over a vaft multitude of *Flemings, Walloons,* and *Dutch*, who with their whole Families fettled at *Norwich*, at *Ipfwich, Colchefter, Canterbury, Exeter,* and the like. From thefe came the *Walloon* Church at *Canterbury*, and the *Dutch* Churches *Norwich, Colchefter* and *Yarmouth*; from hence came the True born *Englifh* Families at thofe Places with Foreign Names; as the *DeVinks* at *Norwich*, the *Rebows* at *Colchefter*, the *Papilons*, &c. at *Canterbury*, Families to whom this Nation are much in debt for the firft planting thofe Manufactures, from which we have fince rais'd the greateft Trades in the World.

This wife Queen knew that number of Inhabitants are the Wealth and Strength of a Nation, fhe was far from that Opinion, we have of late fhown too much of in complaining that Foreigners came to take the Bread out of our Mouths, and ill treating on that account the *French* Proteftants who fled hither for Refuge in the late Perfecution.

Some have faid that above 50000 of them fettled here, and would have made it a Grievance, tho' without doubt 'tis eafie to make it appear that 500000 more would be both ufeful and profitable to this Nation.

Upon

Upon the fetling of thefe Forreigners, the Scale of Trade vifi-bly turn'd both here and in *Flanders*.

The *Flemings* taught our Women and Children to Spin, the Youth to Weave, the Men entred the Loom to labour inftead of going abroad to feek their Fortunes by the War, the feveral Trades of *Bayes* at *Colchefter*, *Sayes* and *Perpets*, at *Sudbury*, *Ipfwich*, &c. *Stuffs* at *Norwich*, *Serges* at *Exeter*, *Silks* at *Canterbury*, and the like, began to flourifh. All the Counties round felt the Profit, the Poor were fet to Work, the Traders gain'd Wealth, and Multitudes of People flock'd to the feveral Parts where thefe Manufactures were erected for Employment, and the Growth of *England*, both in Trade, Wealth and People fince that time, as it is well known to this Honourable Houfe ; fo the Caufes of it ap-pear to be plainly the Introducing of thefe Manufactures, and no-thing elfe.

Nor was the Gain made here by it more vifible than the lofs to the *Flemings*, from hence, and not as is vainly fuggefted from the building the *Dutch* Fort of *Lillo* on the *Scheld*, came the De-cay of that flourifhing City of *Antwerp*. From hence it is plain the *Flemings*, an Induftrious Nation, finding their Trade ruin'd at once, turn'd their Hands to other things, as making of *Lace*, *Linnen*, and the like, and the *Dutch* to the Sea Affairs and Fifh-ing.

From hence they become *Poor*, thin of People, and *weak* in Trade, the Flux both of their Wealth and Trade, running wholly into *England*.

I humbly crave leave to fay, this long Introduction fhall not be thought ufelefs, when I fhall bring it home by the Procefs of thefe Papers to the Subject now in hand, *viz. The Providing for and Employing the Poor.*

Since the Times of *Queen Elizabeth* this Nation has gone on to a Prodigy of Trade, of which the Encreafe of our Cuftoms from 400000 Crowns to two Millions of Pounds Sterling, *per Ann*. is a Demonftration beyond the Power of Argument ; and that this whole Encreafe depends upon, and is principally occafion'd by the encreafe of our Manufacturers is fo plain, I fhall not take up any room here to make it out.

Having

Having thus given an Account how we came to be a rich, flou-rifhing and populous Nation, I crave leave as concifely as I can to examine how we came to be Poor again, if it muft be granted that we are fo.

By Poor here I humbly defire to be underftood, not that we are a poor Nation in general; I fhould undervalue the bounty of Heaven to *England*, and act with lefs Underftanding than moft Men are Mafters of, if I fhould not own, that in general we are *as Rich a Nation* as any in the World; but by Poor I mean burthen'd with a crowd of clamouring, unimploy'd, unprovided for poor People, who make the Nation uneafie, burthen the Rich, clog our Parifhes, and make themfelves worthy of Laws, and peculiar Management to difpofe of and direct them how thefe came to be thus is the Queftion.

And firft I humbly crave leave to lay thefe Heads down as fundamental Maxims, which I am ready at any time to Defend and make out.

1. *There is in* England *more Labour than Hands to perform it, and confequently a want of People, not of Employment.*
2. *No Man in* England, *of found Limbs and Senfes, can be Poor meer-ly for want of Work.*
3. *All our Work-houfes, Corporations and Charities for employing the Poor, and fetting them to Work, as now they are employ'd, or any Acts of Parliament to empower Overfeers of Parifhes, or Parifhes themfelves, to employ the Poor, except as fhall be hereafter excepted, are, and will be publick Naufances, Mifchiefs to the Nation which ferve to the Ruin of Families, and the Encreafe of the Poor.*
4. *That 'tis a Regulation of the Poor that is wanted in* England, *not a fetting them to Work.*

If after thefe things are made out, I am enquir'd of what this Regulation fhould be, I am no more at a lofs to lay it down than I am to affirm what is above; and fhall always be ready, when call'd to it, to make fuch a Propofal to this Honourable Houfe, as with their Concurrence fhall for ever put a ftop to Poverty and Beg-gery, Parifh Charges, Affeffments and the like, in this Nation.

If fuch offers as thefe fhall be flighted and rejected, I have the Satisfaction of having difcharg'd my Duty, and the Confequence muft be, that complaining will be continued in our Streets.

'Tis

'Tis my misfortune, that while I study to make every Head so concise, as becomes me in things to be brought before so Honourable and August an Assembly, I am oblig'd to be short upon Heads that in their own Nature would very well admit of particular Volumes to explain them.

1. I affirm, *That in* England *there is more Labour than Hands to perform it.* This I prove,

1st. From the dearness of Wages, which in *England* out goes all Nations in the World ; and *I know no greater Demonstration in Trade.* Wages, like Exchanges, Rise and Fall as the Remitters and Drawers, the Employers and the Work-men, Ballance one another.

The Employers are the Remitters, the Work-men are the Drawers, if there are more Employers than Work-men, the price of Wages must Rise, because the Employer wants that Work to be done more than the Poor Man wants to do it, if there are more Work-men than Employers the price of Labour falls, because the Poor Man wants his Wages more than the Employer wants to have his Business done.

Trade, like all Nature, most obsequiously obeys the great Law of Cause and Consequence; and this is the occasion why even all the greatest Articles of Trade follow, and as it were pay Homage to this seemingly Minute and Inconsiderable Thing, *The poor Man's Labour.*

I omit, with some pain, the many very useful Thoughts that occur on this Head, to preserve the Brevity I owe to the Dignity of that Assembly I am writing to. But I cannot but Note how from hence it appears, that the Glory, the Strength, the Riches, the Trade, and all that's valuable in a Nation, as to its Figure in the World, depends upon the Number of its People, be they never so mean or poor ; the consumption of Manufactures encreases the Manufacturers; the number of Manufacturers encreases the Consumption; Provisions are consum'd to feed them, Land Improv'd, and more Hands employ'd to furnish Provision: All the Wealth of the Nation, and all the Trade is produc'd by Numbers of People ; but of this by the way.

The price of Wages not only determines the Difference between the Employer and the Work-man, but it rules the Rates of every Market. If Wages grows high, Provisions rise in Proportion, and

I

I humbly conceive it to be a miftake in thofe People, who fay Labour in fuch parts of *England* is cheap becaufe Provifions are cheap, but 'tis plain, Provifions are cheap there becaufe Labour is cheap, and Labour is cheaper in thofe Parts than in others; becaufe being remoter from *London* there is not that extraordinary Difproportion between the Work and the Number of Hands; there are more Hands, and confequently Labour cheaper.

'Tis plain to any obferving Eye, that there is an equal plenty of Provifions in feveral of our South and Weftern Counties, as in *Yorkfhire*, and rather a greater, and I believe I could make it out, that a poor labouring Man may live as cheap in *Kent* or *Suffex* as in the Bifhoprick of *Durham*; and yet in *Kent* a poor Man fhall earn 7 *s*. 10 *s*. 9 *s*. a Week, and in the North 4 *s*. or perhaps lefs; the difference is plain in this, that in *Kent* there is a greater want of People, in Proportion to the Work there, than in the North.

And this on the other hand makes the People of our northen Countries fpread themfelves fo much to the South, where Trade, War and the Sea carrying off fo many, there is a greater want of Hands.

And yet 'tis plain there is Labour for the Hands which remain in the North, or elfe the Country would be depopulated, and the People come all away to the South to feek Work; and even in *Yorkfhire*, where Labour is cheapeft, the People can gain more by their Labour than in any of the Manufacturing Countries of *Germany*, *Italy* or *France*, and live much better.

If there was one poor Man in *England* more than there was Work to employ, either fomebody elfe muft ftand ftill for him, or he muft be ftarv'd; if another Man ftands ftill for him he wants a days Work, and goes to feek it, and by confequence fupplants another, and this a third, and this Contention brings it to this; no fays the poor Man, *That is like to be put out of his Work*, rather than that Man fhall come in I'll do it cheaper; nay, fays the other, but I'll do it cheaper than you; and thus one poor Man wanting but a Days work would bring down the price of Labour in a whole Nation, for the Man cannot ftarve, and will work for any thing rather than want it.

It may be Objected here, This is contradicted by our Number of Beggars.

I am forry to fay I am oblig'd here to call begging an Employment, fince 'tis plain, if there is more Work than Hands to perform it, it, no Man that has his *Limbs* and his *Senses* need to beg, and those that *have not* ought to be put into a Condition not to want it.

So that begging is a meer scandal in the General; *in the Able* 'tis a scandal upon their Industry, and *in the Impotent* 'tis a scandal upon the Country.

Nay, the begging, as now practic'd, is a scandal upon our Charity, and perhaps the foundation of all our present Grievance---- How can it be possible that any Man or Woman, who being found in Body and Mind, may as 'tis apparent they may, have Wages for their Work, should be so base, so meanly spirited, as to beg an Alms for God-sake---- Truly the scandal lies on our Charity; and People have such a Notion in *England* of being pittiful and charitable, that they encourage Vagrants, and by a mistaken Zeal do more harm than good.

This is a large Scene, and much might be said upon it; I shall abridge it as much as possible----. The Poverty of *England* does not lye among the craving Beggars but among poor Families, where the Children are numerous, and where Death or Sickness has depriv'd them of the Labour of the Father; these are the Houses that the Sons and Daughters of Charity, if they would order it well, should seek out and relieve; an Alms ill directed may be Charity to the particular Person, but becomes an Injury to the Publick, and no Charity to the Nation. As for the craving Poor, I am perswaded I do them no wrong when I say, that if they were Incorporated they would be the richest Society in the Nation; and the reason why so many pretend to want Work is, that they can live so well with the pretence of wanting Work, they would be mad to leave it and Work in earnest; and I affirm of my own knowledge, when I have wanted a Man for labouring work, and offer'd 9 s. *per* Week to strouling Fellows at my Door, they have frequently told me to my Face, they could get more a begging, and I once set a lusty Fellow in the Stocks for making the Experiment.

I shall, in its proper place, bring this to a Method of Tryal, since nothing but Demonstration will affect us, 'tis an easie matter to prevent begging in *England*, and yet to maintain all our Impotent Poor at far less charge to the Parishes than they now are oblig'd to be at.

When Queen *Elizabeth* had gain'd her Point as to Manufactories

in

in *England*, fhe had fairly laid the Foundation, fhe thereby found out the way how every Family might live upon their own Labour, like a wife Princefs fhe knew 'twould be hard to force People to Work when there was nothing for them to turn their Hands to; but affoon as fhe had brought the matter to bear, and there was Work for every body that had no mind to ftarve, then fhe apply'd her felf to make Laws to oblige the People to do this Work, and to punifh Vagrants, and make every one live by their own Labour; all her Succeffors followed this laudable Example, and from hence came all thofe Laws againft fturdy Beggars, Vagabonds, Stroulers, &c. which had they been feverely put in Execution by our Magiftrates, 'tis prefum'd thefe Vagrant Poor had not fo encreas'd upon us as they have.

And it feems ftrange to me, from what juft Ground we proceed now upon other Methods, and fancy that 'tis now our Bufinefs to find them Work, and to Employ them rather than to oblige them to find themfelves Work and go about it.

From this miftaken Notion come all our Work-houfes and Corporations, and the fame Error, with fubmiffion, I prefume was the birth of this Bill now depending, which enables every Parifh to erect the Woollen Manufacture within it felf, for the employing their own Poor.

'Tis the miftake of this part of the Bill only which I am enquiring into, and which I endeavour to fet in a true light.

In all the Parliaments fince the Revolution, this Matter has been before them, and I am juftified in this attempt by the Houfe of Commons having frequently appointed Committees to receive Propofals upon this Head.

As my Propofal is General, I prefume to offer it to the General Body of the Houfe, if I am commanded to explain any part of it, I am ready to do any thing that may be ferviceable to this great and noble Defign.

As the former Houfes of Commons gave all poffible Encouragement to fuch as could offer, or but pretend to offer at this needful thing, fo the imperfect Effays of feveral, whether for private or publick Benefit. I do not attempt to determine which have fince been made, and which have obtain'd the Powers and Conditions they have defir'd, have by all their Effects demonftrated the weaknefs of their Defign ; and that they either underftood

not

not the Difeafe, or know not the proper Cure for it.

The Imperfection of all thefe Attempts is acknowledg'd, not only in the Preamble of this new Act of Parliament, but even in the thing, in that there is yet occafion for any new Law.

And having furvey'd, not the neceffity of a new Act, but the Contents of the Act which has been propos'd as a Remedy in this Cafe ; I cannot but offer my Objections againft the Sufficiency of the Propofal, and leave it to the Confideration of this Wife Affembly, and of the whole Nation.

I humbly hope the Learned Gentlemen, under whofe Direction this Law is now to proceed, and by whofe Order it has been Printed, will not think himfelf perfonally concern'd in this Cafe, his Endeavours to promote fo good a Work, as the Relief, Employment, and Settlement of the Poor merit the Thanks and Acknowledgment of the whole Nation, and no Man fhall be more ready to pay his fhare of that Debt to him than my felf. But if his Scheme happen to be fomething fuperficial, if he comes in among the number of thofe who have not fearch'd this Wound to the bottom, if the Methods propos'd are not fuch as will either anfwer his own Defigns or the Nations, I cannot think my felf oblig'd to difpenfe, with my Duty to the Publick Good, to preferve a Perfonal Value for his Judgment, tho' the Gentleman's Merit be extraordinary.

Wherefore, as in all the Schemes I have feen laid for the Poor, and in this Act now before your Honourable Houfe; the general Thought of the Propofers runs upon the Employing the Poor by Work-houfes, Corporations, Houfes of Correction, and the like, and that I think it plain to be feen, that thofe Propofals come vaftly fhort of the main Defign. Thefe Sheets are humbly laid before you, as well to make good what is alledg'd, *viz.* That all thefe Work-houfes, &c. Tend to the Encreafe, and not the Relief of the Poor, as to make an humble Tender of mean plain, but I hope, rational Propofals for the more effectual Cure of this grand Difeafe.

In order to proceed to this great Challenge, I humbly defire the Bills already pafs'd may be review'd, the Practice of our Corporation Work-houfes, and the Contents of this propofed Act examin'd.

In

In all thefe it will appear that the Method chiefly propofed for the Employment of our Poor, is by fetting them to Work on the feveral Manufactures before mention'd ; as *Spinning, Weaving,* and Manufacturing our *Englifh Wool.*

All our Work-houfes, lately Erected in *England,* are in general thus Employ'd, for which without enumerating Particulars, I humbly appeal to the Knowledge of the feveral Members of this Honourable Houfe in their refpective Towns where fuch Corporations have been erected.

In the prefent Act now preparing, as Printed by Direction of a Member of this Honourable Houfe, it appears, *that in order to fet the Poor to Work, it fhall be Lawful for the Overfeers of* every *Town, or of one or more* Towns joyn'd together to *occupy any Trade, Myftery,* &c. *And raife Stocks for the carrying them on for the fetting the Poor at Work, and for the purchafing Wool, Iron, Hemp, Flax, Thread, or other Materials for that Purpofe. Vide the Act Publifh'd by Sir* Humphry Mackworth.

And that Charities given fo and fo, and not exceeding 200 *l. per Annum* for this Purpofe, fhall be Incorporated of Courfe for thefe Ends.

In order now to come to the Cafe in hand, *it is neceffary to premife,* that the thing now in debate is not the Poor of this or that particular Town. The Houfe of Commons are acting like themfelves, as they are the Reprefentatives of all the Commons of *England,* 'tis the Care of all the Poor of *England* which lies before them, not of this or that particular Body of the Poor.

In proportion to this great Work, I am to be underftood that thefe Work-houfes, Houfes of Correction, and Stocks to Employ the Poor may be granted to leffen the Poor in this or that particular part of *England*; and we are particularly told of that at *Briftol,* that it has been fuch a Terror to the Beggars that none of the ftouling Crew will come near the City. But all this allow'd, in general, 'twill be felt in the main, and the end will be au Encreafe of our Poor.

1. The Manufactures that thefe Gentlemen Employ the Poor upon, are all fuch as are before exercis'd in *England.*

2. They are all fuch as are manag'd to a full Extent, and the prefent Accidents of War and Forreign Interruption of Trade confider'd rather beyond the vent of them than under it.

Sup-

Suppose now a Work-house for Employment of Poor Children, sets them to spinning of Worsted.---For every Skein of Worsted these Poor Children Spin, there must be a Skein the less Spun by some poor Family or Person that spun it before ; suppose the Manufacture of making Bays to be erected in *Bishopsgate-street*, unless the Makers of these Bays can at the same time find out a Trade or Consumption for more Bays than were made before. For every piece of Bays so made in *London* there must be a Piece the less made at *Colchester*.

I humbly appeal to the Honourable House of Commons what this may be call'd, and with submission, I think it is nothing at all to Employing the Poor, since 'tis only the transposing the Manufacture from *Colchester* to *London*, and taking the Bread out of the Mouths of the Poor of *Essex* to put it into the Mouths of the Poor of *Middlesex*.

If these worthy Gentlemen, who show themselves so commendably forward to Relieve and Employ the Poor, will find out some new Trade, some new Market, where the Goods they make shall be sold, where none of the same Goods were sold before ; if they will send them to any place where they shall not interfere with the rest of that Manufacture, or with some other made in *England*, then indeed they will do something worthy of themselves, and may employ the Poor to the same glorious Advantage as Queen *Elizabeth* did, to whom this Nation, as a trading Country, owes its peculiar Greatness.

If these Gentlemen could establish a Trade to *Muscovy* for *English* Serges, or obtain an Order from the *Czar*, that all his Subjects should wear Stockings who wore none before, every poor Child's Labour in Spining and Knitting those Stockings, and all the Wool in them would be clear gain to the Nation, and the general Stock would be improved by it, because all the growth of our Country, and all the Labour of a Person who was Idle before, is so much clear Gain to the General Stock.

If they will Employ the Poor in some Manufacture which was not made in *England* before, or not bought with some Manufacture made here before, then they offer at something extraordinary.

But to set Poor People at Work, on the same thing which other poor People were employ'd on before, and at the same time not encrease the Consumption, is giving to one what you take
away

away from another; enriching one poor Man to starve another, putting a Vagabond into an honest Man's Employment, and putting his Diligence on the Tenters to find out some other Work to maintain his Family.

As this is not at all profitable, so *with Submission for the Expression*, I cannot say 'tis honest, because 'tis transplanting and carrying the poor Peoples Lawful Employment from the Place where was their Lawful Settlement, and the hardship of this *our Law consider'd* is intolerable. For Example.

The Manufacture of making Bays is now Establish'd at *Colchester* in *Essex*, suppose it should be attempted to be Erected in *Middlesex*, as a certain Worthy and Wealthy Gentleman near *Hackney* once propos'd, it may be suppos'd if you will grant the Skill in Working the same, and the Wages the same, that they must be made cheaper in *Middlesex* than in *Essex*, and cheapness certainly will make the Merchant buy here rather than there, and so in time all the Bay making at *Colchester* Dyes, and the Staple for that Commodity is remov'd to *London*.

What must the Poor of *Colchester* do, there they buy a Parochial Settlement, those that have numerous Families cannot follow the Manufacture and come up to *London*, for our Parochial Laws Impower the Church-wardens to refuse them a Settlement, so that they are confin'd to their own Countrey, and the Bread taken out of their Mouths, and all this to feed Vagabonds, and to set them to Work, who by their choice would be idle, and who merit the Correction of the Law.

There is another Grievance which I shall endeavour to touch at, which every Man that wishes well to the Poor does not foresee, and which, with humble Submission to the Gentlemen that contriv'd this Act, I see no notice taken of.

There are Arcanas in Trade, which though they are the Natural Consequences of Time and casual Circumstances, are yet become now so Essential to the Publick Benefit, that to alter or disorder them would be an irreparable Damage to the Publick.

I shall explain my self as concisely as I can.

The Manufactures of *England* are happily settled in different Corners of the Kingdom, from whence they are mutually convey'd by a Circulation of Trade to *London* by Wholesale, like the Blood to the Heart, and from thence disperse in lesser quantities to the other parts of the Kingdom by Retail. For Example.

Serges are made at *Exeter, Taunton*, &c. Stuffs at *Norwich*; *Bays*, *Sayes*, *Shaloons*, &c. at *Colchester, Bocking, Sudbury*, and Parts adjacent, Fine Cloath in *Somerset, Wilts, Gloucester* and *Worcestershire*, Course Cloath in *Yorkshire, Kent, Surry*, &c. Druggets at *Farnham, New-bury*, &c. All these send up the Gross of their Quantity to *London*, and receive each others Sorts in Retail for their own use again. *Norwich* Buys *Exeter* Serges, *Exeter* Buys *Norwich* Stuffs; all at *London, Yorkshire* Buys Fine Cloths, and *Gloucester* Course, still at *London*; and the like, of a vast Variety of our Manufactures.

By this Exchange of Manufactures abundance of Trading Families are maintain'd by the Carriage and Re-carriage of Goods, vast number of Men and Cattle are employed, and numbers of Inholders, Victuallers, and their Dependencies subsisted.

And on this account I cannot but observe to your Honours, and 'tis well worth your Consideration, that the already Transposing a vast Woollen Manufacture from several Parts of *England* to *London*, is a manifest detriment to Trade in general, the several Woollen Goods now made in *Spittlefields*, where within this few Years were none at all made, has already visibly affected the several Parts, where they were before made, as *Norwich, Sudbury, Farnham*, and other Towns, many of whose Principal Tradesmen are now remov'd hither, employ their Stocks here, employ the Poor here, and leave the Poor of those Countries to shift for Work.

This Breach of the Circulation of Trade must necessarily Distemper the Body, and I crave leave to give an Example or two.

I'll presume to give an Example in Trade, which perhaps the Gentlemen concern'd in this Bill may, without Reflection upon their knowledge, be ignorant of.

The City of *Norwich*, and parts adjacent, were for some Ages employ'd in the Manufactures of Stuffs and Stockings.

The Latter Trade, which was once considerable, is in a manner wholly transpos'd into *London*, by the vast quanties of worsted Hose Wove by the Frame, which is a Trade within this 20 Years almost wholly new.

Now as the knitting Frame perform that in a Day which would otherwise employ a poor Woman eight or ten Days, by consequence a few Frames perform'd the Work of many Thousand poor People; and the Consumption being not increased, the Effect immediately

mediately appear'd; so many Stockings as were made in *London* so many the fewer were demanded from *Norwich*, till in a few Years the Manufacture there wholly funk, the Mafters there turn'd their hands to other Bufinefs; and whereas the Hofe-Trade from *Norfolk* once return'd at leaft 5000 *s. per* Week, and as fome fay twice that Sum, 'tis not now worth naming.

'Tis in fewer Years, and near our Memory, that of *Spittle-fields* Men have fallen into another branch of the *Norwich* Trade, *viz.* making of Stuffs, Drugets, &c.

If any Man fay the People of *Norfolk* are yet full of Employ, and do not Work; and fome have been fo weak as to make that Reply, avoiding the many other Demonftrations which could be given, this is paft anfwering, *viz.* That the Combers of Wool in *Norfolk* and *Suffolk*, who formerly had all, or ten Parts in eleven of their Yarn Manufactur'd in the Country, now comb their Wool indeed, and fpin the Yarn in the Country, but fend vaft Quanties of it to *London* to be woven; will any Man queftion whether this be not a Lofs to *Norwich*; Can there be as many Weavers as before? And are there not abundance of Work-men and Mafters too remov'd to *London*?

If it be fo at *Norwich*, *Canterbury* is yet more a melancholy Inftance of it, where the Houfes ftand empty, and the People go off, and the Trade dye, becaufe the Weavers are follow'd the Manufacture to *London*; and whereas there was within few Years 200 broad Looms at Work, I am well affur'd there are not 50 now Employ'd in that City.

Thefe are the Effects of tranfpofing Manufactures, and interrupting the Circulation of Trade.

All Methods to bring our Trade to be manag'd by fewer hands than it was before, are in themfelves pernicious to *England* in general, as it leffens the Employment of the Poor, unhinges their Hands from the Labour, and tends to bring our Hands to be fuperior to our Employ, which as yet it is not.

In *Dorfetfhire* and *Somerfetfhire* there always has been a very confiderable Manufacture for Stockings, at *Colchefter* and *Sudbury* for Bayes, Sayes, &c. moft of the Wool thefe Countries ufe is bought at *London*, and carried down into thofe Counties, and then the Goods being Manufactur'd are brought back to *London* to Market; upon tranfpofing the Manufacture as before, all the poor People

and

and all the Cattel who hitherto were Employ'd in that *Voiture,* are
immediately disbanded by their Country, the Inkeepers on the
Roads muſt Decay, ſo much Land lye for other uſes, as the Cattle
Employ'd, Houſes and Tenement on the Roads, and all their Dependencies ſink in Value.

'Tis hard to calculate what a blow it would be to Trade in general, ſhould every County but Manufacture all the ſeveral ſorts
of Goods they uſe, it would throw our Inland Trade into ſtrange
Convulſions, which at preſent is perhaps, or has been, in the great-
eſt Regularity of any in the World.

What ſtrange Work muſt it then make when every Town ſhall
have a Manufacture, and every Pariſh be a Ware-houſe ; Trade
will be burthen'd with Corporations, which are generally equally
deſtructive as Monopolies, and by this Method will eaſily be made ſo.

Pariſh Stocks, under the Direction of Juſtices of Peace, may ſoon
come to ſet up petty Manufactures, and here ſhall all uſeful things
be made, and all the poorer ſort of People ſhall be aw'd or byaſs'd
to Trade there only. Thus the Shop-keepers, who pay Taxes,
and are the Support of our inland Circulation, will immediately
be ruin'd, and thus we ſhall beggar the Nation to provide for the
Poor.

As this will make every Pariſh a Market Town, and every Hoſ-
pital a Store-houſe, ſo in *London,* and the adjacent Parts, to which
vaſt quantities of the Woollen Manufacture will be thus tranſplan-
ted thither, will in time too great and diſproportion'd Numbers
of the People aſſemble.

Tho' the ſettled Poor can't remove, yet ſingle People will ſtroul
about and follow the Manufacturer ; and thus in time ſuch vaſt
numbers will be drawn about *London,* as may be inconvenient to the
Government, and eſpecially Depopulating to thoſe Countries where
the numbers of People, by reaſon of theſe Manufactures are very
conſiderable.

An eminent Inſtance of this we have in the preſent Trade to *Muſ-*
covy, which however deſign'd for an Improvement to the *Engliſh*
Nation, and boaſted of as ſuch, appears to be Converted into a Mo-
nopoly, and proves Injurious and Deſtructive to the Nation. The
Perſons concern'd removing and carrying out our People to teach
that unpoliſh'd Nation the Improvements they are capable of.

If

If the bringing the *Flemings* to *England* brought with them their Manufacture and Trade, carrying our People abroad, especially to a Country where the People work for little or nothing, what may it not do towards Instructing that populous Nation in such Manufactures as may in time tend to the destruction of our Trade, or the reducing our Manufacture to an Abatement in Value, which will be felt at home by an abatement of Wages, and that in Provisions, and that in Rent of Land; and so the general Stock sinks of Course.

But as this is preparing, by eminent Hands, to be laid before this House as a Grievance meriting your Care and Concern, I omit insisting on it here.

And this removing of People is attended with many Inconveniencies which are not easily perceived, as

1. The immediate fall of the Value of all Lands in those Countries where the Manufactures were before; for as the numbers of People, by the Consumption of Provisions, must where ever they encrease make Rents rise, and Lands valuable; so those People removing, tho' the Provisions would, if possible, follow them, yet the Price of them must fall by all that Charge they are at for Carriage, and consequently Lands must fall in Proportion.

2. This Transplanting of Families, in time, would introduce great and new Alterations in the Countries they removed to, which as they would be to the Profit of some Places, would be to the Detriment of others, and can by no means be just any more than it is convenient; for no wise Government studies to put any Branch of their Country to any particular Disadvantages, tho' it may be found in the general Account in another Place.

If it be said here will be Manufactures in every Parish, and that will keep the People at home,

I humbly represent what strange Confusion and particular Detriment to the general Circulation of Trade *mention'd before* it must be, to have every Parish make its own Manufactures.

1. It will make our Towns and Counties independent of one another, and put a damp to Correspondence, which all will allow to be a great Motive of Trade in general.

2. It will fill us with various sorts and kinds of Manufactures, by which our stated sorts of Goods will in time dwindle away in Reputation, and Foreigners not know them one from another.

Our

Our several Manufactures are known by their respective Names ; and our Serges, Bayes and other Goods, are bought abroad by the Character and Reputation of the Places where they are made ; when there shall come new and unheard of Kinds to Market, some better, some worse, as to besure new Undertakers will vary in kinds, the Dignity and Reputation of the *English* Goods abroad will be lost, and so many Confusions in Trade must follow , as are too many to repeat.

3. Either our Parish-stock must sell by Wholesale or by Retail, or both ; if the first, 'tis doubted they will make sorry work of it, and having other Business of their own make but poor Merchants ; if by Retail, then they turn Pedlars, will be a publick nusance to Trade, and at last quite ruin it.

4. This will ruin all the Carriers in *England*, the Wool will be all Manufactured where it is sheer'd, every body will make their own Cloaths, and the Trade which now lives by running thro' a multitude of Hands, will go then through so few, that thousands of Families will want Employment, and this is the only way to reduce us to the Condition spoken of, to have more Hands than Work.

'Tis the excellence of our *English* Manufacture, that it is so planted as to go thro' as many Hands as 'tis possible ; he that contrives to have it go thro' fewer, ought at the same time to provide Work for the rest---- As it is it Employs a great multitude of People, and can employ more ; but if a considerable number of these People be unhing'd from their Employment, it cannot but be detrimental to the whole.

When I say we could employ more People in *England*, I do not mean that we cannot do our Work with those we have, but I mean thus:

First, It should be more People brought over from foreign Parts. I do not mean that those we have should be taken from all common Employments and put to our Manufacture ; we may unequally dispose of our Hands, and so have too many for some Works, and too few for others ; and 'tis plain that in some parts of *England* it is so, what else can be the reason, why in our Southern Parts of *England*, *Kent* in particular, borrows 20000 People of other Counties to get in her Harvest.

But

But if more Forreigners came among us, if it were 2 Millions, it could do us no harm, becaufe they would confume our Provifions, and we have Land enough to produce much more than we do, and they would confume our Manufactures, and we have Wool enough for any Quantity.

I think therefore, with fubmiffion, to erect Manufactures in every Town to tranfpofe the Manufactures from the fettled places into private Parifhes and Corporations, to parcel out our Trade to every Door, it muft be ruinous to the Manufacturers themfelves, will turn thoufands of Families out of their Employments, and take the Bread out of the Mouths of diligent and induftrious Families to feed Vagrants, Thieves and Beggars, who ought much rather to be compell'd, by Legal Methods, to feek that Work which it is plain is to be had ; and thus this Act will inftead of fettling and relieving the Poor, encreafe their Number, and ftarve the beft of them.

It remains now, according to my firft Propofal Page 9. to confider from whence proceeds the Poverty of our People, what Accident, what Decay of Trade, what want of Employment, what ftrange Revolution of Circumftances makes our People Poor, and confequently Burthenfom, and our Laws Deficient; fo as to make more and other Laws Requifite, and the Nation concerned to apply a Remedy to this growing Difeafe. I Anfwer.

1. Not for want of Work ; and befides what has been faid on that Head, I humbly defire thefe two things may be confider'd.

Firft, 'Tis apparent, That if one Man, Woman, or Child, can by his, or her Labour, earn more Money than will fubfift one body, there muft confequently be no want of Work, fince any Man would Work for juft as much as would fupply himfelf rather than ftarve.--- What a vaft difference then muft there be between the Work and the Work-men, when 'tis now known that in *Spittle-fields*, and other adjacent parts of the City, there is nothing more frequent than for a Journey-man Weaver, of many forts, to gain from 15 s. to 30 s. *per* Week Wages, and I appeal to the Silk Throwfters, whether they do not give 8 s. 9 s. and 10 s. *per* Week to blind Men and Cripples, to turn Wheels, and do the meaneft and moft ordinary Works.

Cur

Cur Moriatur Homo, &c.

Why are the Families of thefe Men ftarv'd, and their Children in Work-houfes, and brought up by Charity : I am ready to produce to this Honourable Houfe the Man who for feveral Years has gain'd of me by his handy Labour at the mean fcoundrel Employment of Tile-making from 16 *s.* to 20 *s. per* Week Wages, and all that time would hardly have a pair of Shoes to his Feet, or Cloaths to cover his Nakednefs, and had his Wife and Children kept by the Parifh.

The meaneft Labours in this Nation afford the Work-men fufficient to provide for himfelf and his Family, and that could never be if there was a want of Work.

2. I humbly defire this Honourable Houfe to confider the prefent Difficulty of Raifing Soldiers in this Kingdom ; the vaft Charge the Kingdom is at to the Officers to procure Men ; the many little and *not over honeft Methods* made ufe of to bring them into the Service, the Laws made to compel them ; Why are Goals rumag'd for Malefactors, and the Mint and Prifons for Debtors, the War is an Employment of Honour, and fuffers fome fcandal in having Men taken from the Gallows, and immediately from Villains and Houfebreakers made Gentlemen Soldiers. If Men wanted Employment, and confequently Bread, this could never be, any Man would carry a Mufquet rather than ftarve, and wear the Queens Cloth, or any Bodies Cloth, rather than go Naked, and live in Rags and want ; 'tis plain the Nation is full of People, and 'tis as plain our People have no particular averfion to the War, but they are not poor enough to go abroad; 'tis Poverty makes Men Soldiers, and drives crowds into the Armies, and the Difficulties to get *Englifh*-men to Lift is, becaufe they live in Plenty and Eafe, and he that can earn 20 *s. per* Week at an eafie, fteady Employment, muft be Drunk or Mad when he Lifts for a Soldier, to be knock'd o'th'Head for 3 *s.* 6 *d. per* Week; but if there was no Work to be had, if the Poor wanted Employment, if they had not Bread to eat, nor knew not how to earn it, thoufands of young lufty Fellows would fly to the Pike and Mufquet, and choofe to dye like Men in the Face of the Enemy, rather than lye at home, ftarve, perifh in Poverty and Diftrefs.

From

From all thefe Particulars, and innumerable unhappy Inftances which might be given, 'tis plain, the Poverty of our People which is fo burthenfome, and increafes upon us fo much, does not arife from want of proper Employments, and for want of Work, or Employers, and confequently,

Work-houfes, Corporations, Parifh-ftocks, and the like, to fet them to Work, as they are Pernicious to Trade, Injurious and Impoverifhing to thofe already employ'd, fo they are need-lefs, and will come fhort of the End propos'd.

The Poverty and Exigence of the Poor in *England*, is plainly deriv'd from one of thefe two particular Caufes,

Cafualty or *Crime.*

By Cafualty, I mean Sicknefs of Families, lofs of Limbs or Sight, and any, either Natural or Accidental Impotence as to Labour.

Thefe as Infirmities meerly Providential are not at all concern'd in this Debate; ever were, will, and ought to be the Charge and Care of the Refpective Parifhes where fuch unhappy People chance to live, nor is there any want of new Laws to make Provifion for them, our Anceftors having been always careful to do it.

The Crimes of our People, and from whence their Poverty derives, as the vifible and direct Fountains are,

1. Luxury.
2. Sloath.
3. Pride.

Good Husbandry is no *Englifh* Vertue, it may have been brought over, and in fome Places where it has been planted it has thriven well enough, but 'tis a Forreign Species, it neither loves, nor is belov'd by an *Englifh-man*; and 'tis obferv'd, nothing is fo univerfally hated, nothing treated with fuch a general Contempt as a Rich Covetous Man, tho' he does no Man any Wrong, only faves his own, every Man will have an ill word for him, if a Misfortune happens to him, hang him a covetous old Rogue, 'tis no Matter, he's Rich enough, nay when a certain great Man's Houfe was on Fire, I have heard the People fay one to another, let it burn and 'twill, he's a covetous old miferly Dog, I wo'nt trouble my head to help him, he'd be hang'd before he'd give us a bit of Bread if we wanted it.

Tho'

Tho' this be a Fault, yet I obferve from it fomething of the natural Temper and Genius of the Nation, generally fpeaking, they cannot fave their Money.

'Tis generally faid the *Englifh* get Eftates, and the *Dutch* fave them ; and this Obfervation I have made between Forreigners and *Englifh-men*, that where an *Englifh-man* earns 20 *s. per* Week, and *but juft lives*, as we call it, a *Dutch-man* grows Rich, and leaves his Children in very good Condition ; where an *Englifh* labouring Man with his 9 *s. per* Week lives wretchedly and poor, a *Dutch-man* with that Wages will live very tolerably well, keep the Wolf from the Door, and have every thing handfome about him. In fhort, he will be Rich with the fame Gain as makes the *Englifh-man* poor, he'll thrive when the other goes in Rags, and he'll live when the other ftarves, or goes a begging.

The Reafon is plain, a Man with good Husbandry, and Thought in his Head, brings home his Earnings honeftly to his Family, commits it to the Management of his Wife, or otherwife difpofes it for proper Subfiftance, and this Man with mean Gains lives comfortably, and brings up a Family, when a fingle Man getting the fame Wages, Drinks it away at the Ale-houfe, thinks not of to morrow, layes up nothing for Sicknefs, Age, or Difafter, and when any of thefe happen he's ftarv'd, and a Beggar.

This is fo apparent in every place, that I think it needs no Explication ; that *Englifh* Labouring Peoplo eat and drink, but efpecially the latter three times as much in velue as any fort of Forreigners of the fame Dimenfions in the World.

I am not Writing this as a Satyr on our People, 'tis a fad Truth ; and Worthy the Debate and Application of the Nations Phyfitians Affembled in Parliament, the profufe Extravagant Humour of our poor People in eating and drinking, keeps them low, caufes their Children to be left naked and ftarving, to the care of the Parifhes, whenever either Sicknefs or Difafter befalls the Parent.

The next Article is their *Sloath.*

We are the moft *Lazy Diligent* Nation in the World, vaft Trade, Rich Manufactures, mighty Wealth, univerfal Correfpondence and happy Succefs has been conftant Companions of *England,* and given us the Title of an Induftrious People, and fo in general we are.

But

But there is a general Taint of Slothfulness upon our Poor, there's nothing more frequent, than for an *English-man* to Work till he has got his Pocket full of Money, and then go and be idle, *or perhaps drunk*, till 'tis all gone, and perhaps himself in Debt; and ask him in his Cups what he intends, he'll tell you honeftly, he'll drink as long as it lafts, and then go to work for more.

I humbly fuggeft this Diftemper's fo General, fo Epidemick, and fo deep Rooted in the Nature and Genius of the *Englifh*, that I much doubt it's being eafily redrefs'd, and queftion whether it be poffible to reach it by an Act of Parliament.

This is the Ruine of our Poor, the *Wife mourns*, the Children *ftarves*, the Husband *has Work before him*, but lies at the Ale-houfe, or otherwife *idles away* his time, and won't Work.

'Tis the Men that *wont work*, not the Men that *can get no work*, which makes the numbers of our Poor; all the Work-houfes in *England*, all the Overfeers fetting up Stocks and Manufactures won't reach this Cafe; and I humbly prefume to fay, if thefe two Articles are remov'd, there will be no need of the other.

I make no Difficulty to promife on a fhort Summons, to produce above a Thoufand Families in *England*, within my particular knowledge, who go in Rags, and their Children wanting Bread, whofe Fathers can earn their 15 to 25 *s. per* Week, but will not work, who may have Work enough, but are too idle to feek after it, and hardly vouchfafe to earn any thing more than bare Subfiftance, and Spending Money for themfelves.

I can give an incredible number of Examples in my own Knowledge among our Labouring Poor. I once paid 6 or 7 Men together on a *Saturday* Night, the leaft 10 *s.* and fome 30 *s.* for Work, and have feen them go with it directly to the Ale-houfe, lie there till *Monday*, fpend it every Penny, and run in Debt to boot, and not give a Farthing of it to their Families, tho' all of them had Wives and Children.

From hence comes Poverty, Parifh Charges, and Beggary, if ever one of thefe Wretches falls fick, all they would ask was a Pafs to the Parifh they liv'd at, and the Wife and Children to the Door a Begging.

If this Honourable Houfe can find out a Remedy for this part of the Mifchief; if fuch Acts of Parliament may be made as may effectually cure the Sloth and Luxury of our Poor, that fhall make

Drun-

Drunkards take care of Wife and Children, spendthrifts, lay up for a *wet Day*; Idle, Lazy Fellows Diligent; and Thoughtless Sottish Men, Careful and Provident.

If this can be done, I presume to say there will be no need of transposing and confounding our Manufactures, and the Circulation of our Trade; they will soon find work enough, and there will soon be less Poverty among us, and if this cannot be done, setting them to work upon Woolen Manufactures, and thereby encroaching upon those that now work at them, will but ruine our Trade, and consequently increase the number of the Poor.

I do not presume to offer the Schemes I have now drawn of Methods for the bringing much of this to pass, because I shall not presume to lead a Body so August, so Wise, and so Capable as this Honourable Assembly.

I humbly submit what is here offered, as Reasons to prove the Attempt now making insufficient; and doubt not but in your Great Wisdom, you will find out Ways and Means to set this Matter in a clearer Light, and on a right Foot.

And if this obtains on the House to examine farther into this Matter, the Author humbly recommends it to their Consideration to accept, *in behalf of all the Poor of this Nation*, a Clause in the room of this objected against, which shall answer the End without this terrible Ruin to our Trade and People.

F I N I S.